Original title:
Drifting Delight

Copyright © 2024 Creative Arts Management OÜ
All rights reserved.

Author: Evan Hawthorne
ISBN HARDBACK: 978-9916-90-624-8
ISBN PAPERBACK: 978-9916-90-625-5

Mosaic of Memories upon the Breeze

Whispers in the twilight glow,
Fragments of the past we know.
Colors dance in evening light,
Mosaic dreams take flight tonight.

Echoes of laughter from afar,
Beneath the fading evening star.
Each moment stitched with care,
A tapestry beyond compare.

Swaying leaves tell stories sweet,
Of wanderers we chance to meet.
Time weaves threads of joy and pain,
In every breeze, a memory's chain.

As shadows lengthen, hearts entwine,
In this mosaic, love will shine.
A gentle breeze through branches flies,
Carrying whispers, soft goodbyes.

Seasons Unfolding Like a Silent Dance

Winter whispers soft and clear,
Snowflakes fall, a world austere.
Spring erupts with colors bright,
Petals bloom in sheer delight.

Summer laughs with golden rays,
Laughter echoes, long sun days.
Autumn paints with fiery hues,
Leaves fall down, a gentle muse.

A Tapestry of Sunbeams and Whispering Winds

Sunlight dances on the ground,
Casting shadows all around.
Winds weave tales in gentle flows,
Nature's breath, a soft repose.

Golden threads of light so fine,
Knit the earth like twisted twine.
In the air, a sweet embrace,
Harmony in every space.

Colors of Contentment in the Flowing Stream

Ripples shimmer with the light,
Crystals glisten, pure and bright.
Fish dart under tranquil waves,
Life unfolds in hidden caves.

Breezes carry scents of earth,
Moments pause, a quiet birth.
Colors dance in every bend,
Nature's joy, a perfect blend.

Veils of Mist at Dawn's Whisper

Misty veils caress the morn,
Cloaked in silence, softly borne.
Whispers cling to ancient trees,
Echoes blend with morning breeze.

Light breaks softly, shadows flee,
Morning's kiss, pure poetry.
In the stillness, dreams take flight,
Awakening the world's delight.

A Sanctuary Within Whispering Trees

In the hush of emerald leaves,
Nature speaks in gentle sighs,
Among the roots, a solace lingers,
Where every heartache slowly dies.

Sunbeams filter through the boughs,
Painting shadows on the ground,
Each rustling whisper tells a tale,
Of peace and love that can be found.

The breeze carries sweet perfume,
Of flowers blooming wild and free,
In this refuge, dreams can blossom,
A sanctuary beneath the trees.

Birds serenade the quiet morn,
Their melodies a soft embrace,
Here within this sacred space,
The world fades, leaving no trace.

Lifting Spirits with a Skyward Breath

High above, the azure sprawls,
A canvas vast, where hope ignites,
In every breeze, a call to soar,
To dance with clouds, to chase the lights.

With each inhale, the freedom spreads,
A spirit yearning to expand,
Through open skies, our worries drift,
Like grains of sand in shifting land.

Sun enriches all it touches,
In warmth, our hearts begin to rise,
Feel the lift, as we embrace,
The skyward breath that never lies.

Let go of all that binds you here,
In the heights, we find release,
In every moment, feel the thrill,
As we are cradled, light and peace.

Enchanted Moments Through Open Windows

A gentle breeze rolls through the room,
Carrying whispers of the past,
Through open windows, stories bloom,
In fleeting moments, memories cast.

Sunlight dances on dusty frames,
Illuminating paths we walked,
Each shadow whispers love's sweet names,
In quiet corners, spirits talked.

The scent of rain on cobblestones,
Brings echoes of a day once clear,
In every drop, a song of hope,
As moments linger, ever near.

Through open windows, life unfolds,
With each embrace, a new refrain,
In enchanted times, our hearts reside,
Relishing the joy, devoid of pain.

The Dance of Light on Water's Surface

Amidst the ripples, sunlight twirls,
A ballet on the liquid dance,
Each shimmer weaves a tale of pearls,
In nature's arms, we lose our chance.

Reflections glide like fleeting dreams,
As shadows stretch and softly sway,
In this embrace, the water gleams,
A fleeting moment, bright and gay.

Waves lapping gently at the shore,
Compose a symphony so sweet,
Where day meets night, forevermore,
In the rhythm, our hearts repeat.

With every glimmer, time suspends,
The dance endures, both wild and calm,
As light and water weave their threads,
In serenity, they share a psalm.

Floating Lanterns on Quiet Waters

Gentle glow across the night,
Lanterns drifting, soft and bright.
Whispers of the winds that sway,
Carrying hopes, they'll find their way.

Rippling waters hold their grace,
Reflections dance, a tranquil space.
Promises and dreams take flight,
Wishing stars shine through the night.

Painted Skies of Peaceful Dreams

Brushstrokes linger in the sky,
Colors blend as day drifts by.
Clouds like canvases unfold,
Whispers of stories yet untold.

Twilight glows in shades of blue,
A serene world, fresh and new.
Stars awaken in the haze,
Lighting paths through evening's gaze.

Echoes of Laughter in Gentle Currents

Bubbling streams that softly flow,
Carry laughter, sweet and low.
Whirls of joy through fields of green,
Nature's chorus, bright and keen.

Rippling sounds of life abound,
In every splash, a joyful sound.
Memories float on breezy tides,
With every wave, our spirit glides.

Unraveled Threads of the Day's Canvas

Morning dawns with golden threads,
Weaving dreams upon our beds.
Each moment captures time's embrace,
Colors merge in life's bright face.

As shadows stretch, the light will fade,
In the tapestry we have made.
Night will come, but hope will stay,
For every thread shall guide the way.

Swirls of Color in the Evening Glow

The horizon blushes bright,
As day surrenders to the night.
Streaks of orange, pink, and gold,
Whisper tales of dreams untold.

Clouds dance gently in the breeze,
Painting canvases with ease.
Each hue a story to unfold,
In swirls of color, brave and bold.

Stars peek out, a twinkling cheer,
Emerging secrets, crystal clear.
The night embraces every ray,
In this twilight's gentle play.

With every breath, the colors blend,
A magic spell that seems to mend.
As evening glows, our hearts take flight,
In swirls of color, pure delight.

The Embrace of a Gentle Zephyr

A whisper soft, a tender sigh,
The zephyr comes to say goodbye.
It dances through the swaying trees,
A symphony that brings such ease.

It brushes past with gentle grace,
A fleeting touch, a sweet embrace.
It carries scents of blooming flowers,
Moments treasured through the hours.

The world stands still within its hold,
As stories of the wind are told.
Each rustling leaf, a soft refrain,
In nature's breath, a sweet sustain.

So close your eyes, let worries cease,
In the zephyr's arms, find peace.
With every gust, the heart will soar,
A gentle touch forevermore.

Moments Suspended in Time's Flow

Each heartbeat, a silent refrain,
Moments frozen, joy and pain.
In the stillness, memories glow,
Captured gently in time's flow.

A glance exchanged, a fleeting smile,
Life slows down for just a while.
In laughter shared, in whispers low,
Threads of our story intertwine so.

The ticking clock begins to fade,
As we dance in this serenade.
Each second stretches, soft and slow,
In moments suspended, love will grow.

The sands of time, like grains of light,
Reflect our paths beneath the night.
In every pause, in every show,
We find our truth in time's soft flow.

A Soft Melody Through the Open Air

A tune that drifts on gentle winds,
Through valleys low and mountain bends.
It carries dreams on notes that sway,
A soft melody to lighten the day.

The song of birds at break of dawn,
Awakens life, as shadows yawn.
Each chorus brings a sweet refrain,
In harmony with joy and pain.

With every breeze, the music flows,
In silent whispers, it softly grows.
A lullaby that calms the soul,
Each note, a piece that makes us whole.

So let the melody take flight,
Through open air, beneath the light.
In every heartbeat, let us dare,
To breathe in life, this soft affair.

The Sweet Escape of a Nightingale's Song

In twilight's hush, the nightingale sings,
A melody soft, the heart it wrings.
Under the stars, her voice takes flight,
Carrying dreams through the velvet night.

Among the trees, secrets whisper low,
Echoes of love in the moon's soft glow.
Each note a promise, tender and clear,
A sweet escape from all doubt and fear.

Wandering Paths and Forgotten Dreams

Footsteps echo on the winding way,
Lost in the whispers of yesterday.
Beneath the leaves, where shadows play,
Forgotten dreams in the soft decay.

Through tangled roots and tangled time,
The heart remembers a distant chime.
Each fork in the road, a choice to feel,
Wandering paths that slowly heal.

Embracing Solitude in Nature's Caress

Amidst the woods, where silence reigns,
   I find the peace that solitude claims.
A gentle breeze and the rustling leaves,
   In nature's arms, the spirit weaves.

The stars above, so calm, so bright,
   In their glow, I lose my fright.
Time slows down, the heart takes flight,
   Embracing solitude in the night.

Bubbles of Laughter in the Summer Air

Children play in the golden sun,
Bubbles of laughter, a joyful run.
With each bright pop, a moment shared,
In summer's glow, the world is bared.

Wildflowers dance in the gentle breeze,
Nature smiles among the trees.
Memories made, with love and care,
Bubbles of laughter fill the air.

Weightless Journeys

In silent skies, we drift and soar,
With wings of hope, forevermore.
The world below, a distant hue,
In weightless dreams, I fly with you.

Through clouds that whisper, secrets old,
In gentle winds, our stories told.
We chase the dusk, embrace the dawn,
In every heartbeat, we are drawn.

The stars above, our guiding light,
In endless space, we shine so bright.
Together we'll explore unknown,
In unity, we've always grown.

Afloat in Azure Dreams

Beneath the vast and endless sky,
We drift on currents, you and I.
The ocean's song, a soothing balm,
In azure waves, our hearts feel calm.

The sunlit paths we choose to roam,
In every tide, we find a home.
With every splash, our laughter flows,
In this bright world, our love just grows.

A canvas painted, shades of blue,
In these dreams, I'm lost in you.
Together we sail, side by side,
In azure dreams, our hearts collide.

Gliding Through Gentle Mists

In morning's hush, the mists arise,
A soft embrace, a sweet surprise.
Through silver veils, we gently glide,
In whispered winds, our fears subside.

The world transformed, a dreamlike scene,
In twilight's glow, we feel serene.
With every step, the earth is light,
Through gentle mists, we take our flight.

Each breath a moment, soft and clear,
With you beside, I've naught to fear.
We dance among the fading light,
In mists that cradle day and night.

A Dance with Distant Stars

In velvet skies, we find our place,
With galaxies that weave in grace.
Each twinkling light, a dream's embrace,
In cosmic realms, we leave a trace.

With every wish upon a star,
We journey near, we journey far.
In swirling realms of bright delight,
Our souls unite, a wondrous sight.

Through ages past, our spirits soar,
In endless dance, we crave for more.
Together beneath celestial tides,
With distant stars, our love abides.

Glimmers of Hope on the Horizon

In the twilight's gentle glow,
Whispers dance on the breeze.
Promises held in the shadows,
A night that softly frees.

Stars emerge like distant dreams,
Guiding hearts toward the light.
With every flicker, it seems,
Hope ignites the dark night.

Faint refrains of laughter rise,
Carried far on soft air.
In the silence, truth replies,
Revealing the world we share.

As dawn breaks the spell of night,
Colors bloom with the sun.
In each glimmer, we take flight,
A new day has begun.

Wandering Through Fields of Dandelion Wishes

In a meadow lush and wide,
Dandelions sway and dance.
Each wish carried by the tide,
Offering a fleeting chance.

Softly drifting on the breeze,
Petals spin like gentle dreams.
Nature calls us to our knees,
Where sunlight softly gleams.

Starlit hopes on windswept nights,
A magic spun from the past.
Every sigh ignites our flights,
Memories that hold us fast.

Through fields where the wild hearts play,
Adventure whispers near.
With each step, we find our way,
Blooming joy without fear.

Colors of Infinity in an Open Sky

Above the hills, a canvas spread,
With hues that blend and swirl.
The sky sings tales long unsaid,
In a vibrant dance, we twirl.

From sapphire to scarlet red,
Infinite dreams reside.
In every stroke, our spirits tread,
Curious hearts open wide.

Clouds drifting like soft-spun lace,
Reflecting sunlight's embrace.
Each color holds a sacred space,
A journey we all chase.

As evening paints with strokes of gold,
The horizon wears a crown.
In these moments, both brave and bold,
We weave life's tapestry down.

Ripples of Joy in the Fabric of Time

In the stillness, moments flare,
Ripples dance in the night.
Glistening echoes whisper fair,
Inviting us to take flight.

Each heartbeat a note in the song,
Threads woven through our days.
In the tapestry, we belong,
As love's warm light displays.

Memories etched like starlit dreams,
Carried on gentle waves.
Time holds laughter's purest beams,
In the joy that it saves.

Through the moments, intertwined,
We find a peace sublime.
With every breath, we are aligned,
In ripples of joy, we climb.

Floating Dreams on a Serene Lake

Beneath the calm, the waters sleep,
Reflections deep, where secrets keep.
Whispers ride the gentle breeze,
As dreams unfold beneath the trees.

Sails of thought drift on the tide,
Each moment pure, a fleeting ride.
In rippled hues, the visions play,
Floating softly, they drift away.

Moonlight dances on the screen,
Serene and bright, a tranquil sheen.
In the silence, hearts align,
Floating dreams, forever mine.

Summoning the stars at night,
In harmony, a stunning sight.
On this lake, we lose our fears,
Floating dreams through endless years.

Celestial Patterns in the Sky

Stars alight in velvet seas,
Whirling tales on cosmic breeze.
Constellations weave and glow,
In depths of night, the wonders flow.

Galaxies twirl, a dancing spree,
Stories told of you and me.
Nebulae, like brushstrokes bright,
Paint the canvas of the night.

In silent awe, we gaze above,
Embracing all that we dream of.
A cosmic path, a stellar guide,
Where every heartache wants to hide.

With each twinkling light we find,
Celestial whispers tightly bind.
Patterns dance in twilight's hue,
In this vast expanse, we're renewed.

A Dance of Clouded Whimsy

Clouds parade in skies of gray,
Fleeting thoughts drift far away.
Soft and light, they twist and turn,
In this dance, our hearts shall yearn.

Shapes of laughter, forms of dreams,
Weaving stories, bursting seams.
A sunbeam slips through cotton white,
Illuminating joyful sights.

Raindrops tap on windowpanes,
Melody in soft refrains.
Watch them swirl with playful grace,
As whims unfold in every space.

In the breeze, the secrets play,
Whispers soft, they'll guide the way.
A dance of clouds, ephemeral,
In the sky, our hearts enthrall.

Waves of Laughter Ride the Current

Surging forth, the waters gleam,
Echoes rise like laughter's dream.
Each wave tells a tale so bright,
In playful rhythm day and night.

Children's giggles on the shore,
Crashing waves, they ask for more.
Salt and sun, a joyous blend,
Where every moment seems to transcend.

Ride the currents, feel the thrill,
As laughter dances, hearts will fill.
Surging tides, the spirit plays,
In this harmony, time decays.

Underneath the setting sun,
Waves of laughter, ever spun.
In the sea of life we find,
Joyful currents, hearts entwined.

Melodies of the Heart in Gentle Waters

Whispers flow through peaceful streams,
Caressing dreams like soft moonbeams.
Hearts entwined in nature's song,
Where love and hope forever belong.

Ripples dance beneath the trees,
Carrying tales upon the breeze.
In every note, a story spins,
Of whispered vows and joyful sins.

Gentle waves, a soothing touch,
In silence, they can say so much.
Life's rhythm sways like tender leaves,
In the calm, the heart believes.

As twilight falls, the colors blend,
A serenade without an end.
In gentle waters, we'll reside,
With melodies of love as our guide.

Canvas of Clouds and Sunlit Smiles

A canvas vast, with hues so bright,
Clouds paint dreams in morning light.
Sunlit smiles on faces show,
A warmth that makes the spirit glow.

In every shade, a story told,
Of laughter shared and love that's bold.
The sky, a masterpiece to behold,
With each new dawn, life's threads unfold.

Whispered wishes drift up high,
Carried softly through the sky.
As daylight fades to night's embrace,
We trace the stars with hope and grace.

So let's create this art divine,
With every moment, yours and mine.
A canvas rich in colors bright,
Where joy and dreams take wondrous flight.

Floating Between the Realms of Wonder

In twilight's glow, we softly drift,
Between the worlds, a precious gift.
A space where dreams and truths collide,
In wonder's arms, we choose to glide.

With every step, the magic grows,
The heart awakens, love bestows.
Curious minds in fields of light,
Explore the dark, embrace the bright.

Floating free on clouds of thought,
In realms of wonder, we are caught.
A dance of stars, a gentle sway,
Inviting hopes to come and play.

As evening falls, we close our eyes,
To dream of worlds that fill the skies.
In whispered dreams, we find our place,
Floating softly in wonder's grace.

Echoes of Light in a Starlit Reverie

In a starlit night, the silence sings,
Echoes of light on shimmering wings.
Whispers of wishes touch the ground,
In this reverie, love is found.

Stars twinkle soft like gentle sighs,
Illuminating dreams that rise.
Every glance, a comet's flight,
Bound together in the night.

With hearts alight, we chase the glow,
Through shadows deep, where secrets flow.
In every beat, a tale retold,
Of warmth and passion pure as gold.

As dawn approaches, dreams hold tight,
In echoes of joy, we feel the light.
A starlit reverie we claim,
With every spark, we fan the flame.

Echoing Laughter on the Waves

Laughter dances on the tide,
As sea foam curls, side by side.
Joyful echoes fill the air,
Nature's song, a vibrant prayer.

Children play on sunlit shores,
Collecting shells, opening doors.
With every splash, a story's spun,
Beneath the warm and glowing sun.

The gulls join in the playful cheer,
Their cries a melody so dear.
Waves rush in, then softly sway,
In this moment, we're at play.

Each ripple hums a carefree tune,
As day surrenders to the moon.
We chase the echoes, set them free,
In laughter shared, we find our glee.

A Symphony of Solitude

In stillness, whispers weave around,
A symphony in silence found.
Each note is soft, yet crystal clear,
Inviting thoughts I've kept so near.

The clock ticks slow, a gentle pace,
In solitude, I find my grace.
A canvas broad, with dreams unfurled,
Within my heart, I paint my world.

The moonlight graces empty floors,
While shadows dance behind closed doors.
Each breath I take, a sacred vow,
To cherish now, to honor how.

With every sigh, I come alive,
In quietude, my spirits thrive.
This symphony, a soft embrace,
In solitude, I've found my place.

Whispers of the Wandering Breeze

The breeze carries secrets untold,
Stories of adventures bold.
It whispers through the swaying trees,
A gentle heart that roams with ease.

Each gust, a message from afar,
Guiding dreams like a shining star.
It twirls around on paths unseen,
Awakening the calm and green.

In every hush, a tale unfolds,
Of wanderlust and freedom's hold.
The air alive with fleeting grace,
Invites the soul to wander space.

Through valleys deep and mountains high,
The breeze will carry you and I.
In whispers soft, we find our way,
As nature sings at end of day.

Ebbing Tides of Joy

Joy ebbs and flows like the sea,
Rising gently, wild and free.
In moments captured, hearts align,
A dance of waves, a sweet design.

Sunrise paints the water gold,
Each glimmer, a story told.
With every surf that breaks and swells,
The heartbeat of the ocean dwells.

As laughter mingles with the spray,
We chase the tides, come what may.
Ebbing low, then soaring high,
In joy, we learn to laugh and sigh.

When night descends, the waves still play,
In dreams that wash the day away.
As tides recede, our spirits grow,
In ebbing joy, we find our flow.

Gliding Through a Canvas of Cloud Nine

Soft clouds embrace the sun's warm glow,
Floating dreams where wild breezes blow.
Whispers of joy in the azure sky,
We dance on air, as moments fly.

Colors blend in a pastel hue,
Hearts soar high, like the lark that flew.
Weightless feeling, we drift and sway,
In this realm, we wish to stay.

Time stands still, a beautiful freeze,
Every heartbeat, a fleeting breeze.
Caught in wonder, in awe we bask,
In the sky's embrace, no need to ask.

Gliding softly through tides of light,
We chase our dreams into the night.
In this rapture, we find our peace,
A canvas of joy that will never cease.

Dreams Carried by a Gentle Tide

On sandy shores, our hopes reside,
Waves caress as the stars collide.
In the moon's glow, whispers arise,
Carried gently, like lullabies.

Each ebb and flow, a tale to tell,
The ocean's heart casts a timeless spell.
With seashells and dreams, we sail away,
Embracing dusk, we greet the day.

In twilight's hush, the world unwinds,
Secrets hidden in watery binds.
We sail beyond to realms unknown,
In the tender tide, we find our home.

The rhythm of waves, a soothing sound,
In their embrace, our dreams are found.
Together afloat, we ride the night,
Carried onward by soft moonlight.

Ballet of the Wind Across Open Plains

Beneath the sky, the whispers dance,
The wind invites to take a chance.
Shadows twirl on the golden grass,
As nature sings, we let time pass.

Graceful breezes swirl all around,
In this waltz, we hear life's sound.
Each gust a call to soar and glide,
In harmony, we take the ride.

With open hearts, we chase the sun,
Across the plains, we laugh and run.
The world a stage, where dreams unfold,
In the ballet, our stories told.

As twilight dims, the dancers slow,
In silence, secrets begin to flow.
Together we stand, as stars ignite,
In the night's embrace, we hold on tight.

Glistening Mornings of Whispered Hopes

On dawn's canvas, dew drops gleam,
Each sparkle holds a whispered dream.
Sunrise breaks, a gentle touch,
Awakening hearts that long so much.

Birds sing softly as skies unfold,
Painting stories both brave and bold.
In the golden light, we find anew,
The promise of a day for me and you.

With every ray, a chance appears,
To conquer doubts and calm our fears.
Hand in hand, we greet the morn,
In every breath, fresh hope is born.

The world alive in vibrant hues,
A tapestry of dreams infused.
In glistening mornings, we rise and shine,
With whispered hopes, our hearts align.

The Gentle Art of Letting Go

In the quiet of the night,
Whispers dance like fading light.
Memories held, now falling free,
Like leaves that drift from the old tree.

With each breath, a piece unbinds,
Hearts release what once confined.
In the soft embrace of change,
Life unfolds, gently rearranged.

The past may linger, but time will show,
The beauty found in letting go.
Trust the journey, trust the flow,
Find the peace in what we sow.

So we learn, with every sigh,
To say farewell and still fly high.
In the art of loss, we find our grace,
A gentle smile upon our face.

A Flight of Fancy through Moonlit Fields

Under the stars, a pathway glows,
A whispering wind, where freedom flows.
Moonlight dances on the dew,
As dreams awaken, fresh and new.

We run through shadows, wild and free,
Chasing echoes of destiny.
With laughter carried by the night,
Our hearts take wing, embracing flight.

In the hush of twilight's grace,
We lose ourselves in time and space.
Each step a rhythm, each breath a song,
Together here is where we belong.

As the moon beams down with gentle light,
We find our purpose, pure delight.
Through fields of hope, we boldly tread,
In fancy's arms, our spirits fed.

Celestial Secrets Beneath Rolling Waves

Beneath the tides, a world unseen,
Where starlit whispers dwell serene.
Secrets held in azure deep,
In silken currents, mysteries sleep.

The ocean breathes with ancient sighs,
As galaxies weave across the skies.
Each ripple holds a tale to tell,
Of cosmic wonders where echoes dwell.

From coral castles to sunken dreams,
Life glimmers softly, or so it seems.
In the dance of water, stars align,
A symphony of the divine.

So dive beneath, let go of fear,
Embrace the magic that draws near.
For in the depths, where shadows play,
Celestial secrets light the way.

Kites Swaying in the Golden Glare

In the meadow, colors soar,
Kites dancing high, forevermore.
With laughter ringing through the air,
Joy takes flight without a care.

Each thread a dream, each tug a wish,
In the sun's warm kiss, we find our bliss.
Upward bound, the skies they grace,
Painting trails in endless space.

With winds that sing a playful tune,
We soar and dip beneath the moon.
In golden glare, our spirits rise,
Chasing freedom through endless skies.

So let them fly, these kites of hope,
In the azure vast, we learn to cope.
With every gust, our hearts align,
Swaying gently, your hand in mine.

Echoes of the Twilight Sky

Whispers of the evening light,
Stars begin their gentle flight.
Shadows dance on the silver ground,
In the dusk, sweet dreams are found.

Colors fade, a soft embrace,
Nighttime sings with calming grace.
Clouds drift by, like thoughts afloat,
Carried on a twilight note.

Fading warmth from day's goodbye,
Echoes of the twilight sky.
Nature's hush, the world at peace,
In this stillness, worries cease.

Silent moments, softly shared,
In the dusk, we're unprepared.
Yet in shadows, hope will grow,
As the night begins to glow.

Drifting on a Feathered Heart

Carried by the softest breeze,
Moments feel like whispered pleas.
Floating on a feathered dream,
Life unfolds, a gentle seam.

Wings of hope, they lift and sway,
Guiding hearts along the way.
In the calm of morning's light,
Life ignites, the spirit's flight.

Tender wishes drift like clouds,
Among the trees, so tall, so proud.
Every heartbeat, light and free,
Drifting on a destiny.

Boundless skies and endless grace,
In this space, we find our place.
With each breath, we soar anew,
Drifting where the skies are blue.

Melodies of the Moonlit Sea

Waves that whisper in the night,
Singing stories, pure delight.
Underneath a silver glow,
Tides embrace the world below.

Each ripple dances, soft and clear,
Melodies that all can hear.
Guided by the moon's kind light,
Secrets held until the night.

Stars reflect on waters deep,
Cradled dreams in azure sleep.
Harmony in every strand,
Melodies from a timeless land.

With each wave, a tale will weave,
In the night, we all believe.
The sea, a song of endless glee,
Melodies set our spirits free.

Featherweight Fantasies

In a world where dreams take flight,
Featherweight, they feel so light.
Every thought, a gentle breeze,
Carrying us through the trees.

Dancing on the edge of night,
Fantasies in soft moonlight.
Imagination paints the sky,
With every whispered, daring lie.

Floating freely, hearts ignite,
In this realm, we chase delight.
Colorful visions, sweet and rare,
Featherweight, beyond compare.

With each flutter, worlds unfold,
Secrets whispered, stories told.
In the skies, we find our way,
Featherweight, where dreams can play.

Serenade for the Floating Heart

In a garden where whispers blend,
Petals drift on the soft, warm air.
The moonlight sings a sweet, soft tune,
As dreams dance lightly, beyond compare.

Each heartbeat echoes through the night,
With shadows cast from stars so bright.
The floating heart in calm embrace,
Finds solace in this sacred space.

Waves of longing crash and swell,
Together in the night, we dwell.
A serenade for souls at play,
As night transforms the dusk to day.

In this moment, time stands still,
The world fades under love's soft thrill.
With every sigh and every glance,
We lose ourselves in night's romance.

Picturesque Paths of Wandering Souls

Beneath the arch of ancient trees,
Two wanderers tread the leaf-strewn way.
Sunlight dapples through the leaves,
Illuminating dreams that sway.

Each step paints a story untold,
A tapestry woven with threads of gold.
Through valleys deep and mountains high,
The paths of souls, they twist and lie.

With laughter carried on the breeze,
They journey on, each heart at ease.
In every shadow, every light,
They find their truth in the endless night.

A time of wonder, a fleeting glance,
In picturesqueness, they find their chance.
To dance beneath the stars so bright,
Two wandering souls, lost in the night.

Ribbons of Light in the Twilight Breeze

Twilight whispers in hues so rare,
As ribbons of light weave through the trees.
A gentle touch, a tender care,
Carried softly on the evening's breeze.

The horizon glows with amber dreams,
Reflecting hope in each shimmering ray.
In the embrace of fading beams,
The heart finds peace at the end of day.

Each breath taken with the stars above,
A moment lost in celestial play.
Ribbons of light dance, speak of love,
In twilight's arms, they forever stay.

As shadows stretch and the world grows still,
Magic lingers in the cooling air.
In this gentle space, hearts are fulfilled,
Wrapped in ribbons, light and care.

Charmed by the Pull of the Open Sea

The salty air sings of adventure,
Whispers of waves lure hearts to roam.
With sails unfurled, we seek the treasure,
As the open sea calls us home.

Beneath the vast and starry dome,
Every tide stirs the souls that yearn.
With every crest, we find our poem,
In each embrace, the heart will burn.

Charmed by the sound of ocean's roar,
We dance upon the shifting sand.
The horizon beckons forevermore,
As we ride the waves, hand in hand.

The pull of the sea, a timeless spell,
In depths unknown, our spirits soar.
Together we chase what the tides will tell,
For in the ocean's heart, we explore.

Whispers on the Breeze

Soft whispers float on gentle air,
Carrying secrets we long to share.
Laughter dances on the sunlit glow,
While time slips by, oh so slow.

Trees sway lightly with stories untold,
In their embrace, treasures unfold.
Nature's breath hums a lullaby sweet,
Inviting all souls to pause, take a seat.

Memories linger like petals in flight,
Bathed in the warmth of fading light.
Every rustle sings of love's refrain,
In whispers we find joy, even in pain.

So let us wander where shadows blend,
In harmony's cradle, our hearts mend.
With whispers on the breeze, we will roam,
Finding in each moment a sense of home.

Celestial Canoes

Under the stars, we sail through dark,
In celestial canoes, we leave our mark.
Tidal waves shift as dreams take flight,
Guided by moons in the velvety night.

Ripples of stardust shimmer and dance,
In the cosmos, we grasp our chance.
Each stroke of the oar brings us near,
To worlds unseen, yet so profoundly clear.

Galaxies whisper tales of old,
In the silence, their wonders unfold.
Time drifts away on the cosmic sea,
In boats of the heavens, we wander free.

With every journey, our spirits rise,
In celestial canoes, we touch the skies.
Dreams cascade like water's embrace,
As starlight guides us through endless space.

Beyond the Tides of Time

Waves whisper softly, calling our name,
Beyond the tides, nothing is the same.
Footprints washed away with every tide,
Yet memories linger, refusing to hide.

Seashells echo the laughter we shared,
In the footprints of time, we boldly dared.
Each glance back holds a hint of the past,
But the future awaits, bright and vast.

Embracing the moment, we ride the flow,
With hearts wide open, ready to grow.
In the tide's embrace, we learn to let go,
As life teaches lessons in ebb and flow.

So we'll sail onward, beyond time's grace,
Finding our rhythm in this sacred space.
With every wave, we dance and align,
Together forever, beyond the sands of time.

Swaying in Sweet Serenity

In the twilight glow, we sway and twine,
Cradled in peace, our hearts align.
Gentle breezes kiss our cheeks so light,
As stars awaken to grace the night.

Whispers of the earth weave a tender song,
Where nature's embrace feels right, not wrong.
Each sigh of the trees tells stories anew,
In this sweet serenity, just me and you.

Clouds drift lazily, painting the skies,
As dreams cascade in the softest sighs.
In each moment, we find our blend,
Swaying together until journeys end.

So let us linger in this fleeting hour,
Basking in love, cultivating power.
With gentle hearts and spirits set free,
We're swaying in sweet serenity.

Petals Carried by the Springtime Gales

Softly drifting through the air,
Petals dance without a care.
Colors bright, a vibrant sight,
Whispers of the warm daylight.

Blossoms twirl on gentle streams,
Basking in the sun's warm beams.
Nature sings a joyful tune,
Heralding the grace of June.

Breezes weave a fragrant spree,
Every bud, a part of me.
In the garden, life takes flight,
With each petal, pure delight.

Catch the beauty, let it soar,
In the springtime, we explore.
Hold the moment, feel the thrill,
As the world begins to heal.

Cascades of Wishes on a Starlit Night

Beneath the canvas of the sky,
Wishes fall like fireflies.
Sparkling dreams in twinkling light,
Guide our hearts through the night.

Cascades echo in the dark,
Each desire, a glowing spark.
Gentle whispers, soft and clear,
Carried far, they disappear.

Moonlight weaves a silver thread,
Entwining thoughts within our head.
Every flicker, every gleam,
Lifts our spirits, starts to dream.

Together, under skies so vast,
Chasing shadows of our past.
Wishes blend in starlit skies,
Carried forth as love replies.

Chasing Shadows in Luminous Fields

In the dusk, the shadows play,
Chasing dreams at end of day.
Luminous fields, a golden hue,
Painting life in shades anew.

Whispers carried on the breeze,
Secrets shared among the trees.
Nature's symphony unfolds,
In the silence, magic holds.

Footprints mark the path we tread,
Chasing shadows, hearts widespread.
With each moment, time stands still,
In the joy, we find our will.

Fields of wonder, wild and free,
Threads of fate entwined in glee.
Chasing shadows, we'll embrace,
Every heartbeat leaves a trace.

Harmony in the Silence of Swaying Grass

In the stillness, whispers grow,
Swaying grass, a gentle flow.
Nature breathes in quiet grace,
Finding peace in this sacred space.

Each blade dances with the breeze,
An orchestra among the trees.
Quiet songs of earth and sky,
Harmonies that wander by.

Underneath the setting sun,
Harmony is never done.
In every rustle, soft and sweet,
A tranquil pulse, a steady beat.

Listen close, let worries pass,
In the silence of the grass.
Find the rhythm, lose your woes,
In life's beauty, love still grows.

Embracing the Soft Horizon

Whispers of dawn greet the day,
Colors blend in a gentle sway,
Horizon stretches wide and bright,
Promises beckon in soft light.

Clouds drift like thoughts in the sky,
Each breeze a tender goodbye,
Mountains stand with arms outstretched,
Holding secrets that haven't yet fetched.

As the sun dips low and slow,
Golden beams start to glow,
Dreams are woven in twilight's thread,
Embracing all that lies ahead.

With every shade, a new embrace,
Nature's canvas finds its place,
In the stillness, hearts will soar,
Embracing life forevermore.

Lost in Luminous Lullabies

Stars twinkle softly in the night,
Melodies born from cosmic light,
Whispers float on the gentle breeze,
Carried along with such sweet ease.

Dreams awaken in silver beams,
Dancing to the truth of dreams,
Moonbeams cradle sleepy eyes,
In a world where magic lies.

Caught in the web of serenade,
Night's embrace, a soft cascade,
Floating through the realms of sleep,
Where secrets of the stars run deep.

Lost in this luminous lullaby,
Time drifts on like a sigh,
Wrapped in the glow, hearts align,
To the song of the divine.

Serenade of the Spheres

Whirling notes in cosmic dance,
Each planet sings, a timeless chance,
Harmony flows through endless space,
A serenade in every place.

Galaxies spin with grace divine,
Echoes of a celestial line,
In the void, where starlights play,
A serenade leads the way.

Comets flash like fleeting dreams,
Chasing whispers of ancient themes,
In the darkness, melodies birth,
Songs that resonate with Earth.

In this cosmic symphony vast,
Time unwinds, present and past,
Together we dance to the spheres,
Lost in the music that endears.

Wandering through Sunlit Skies

Glistening rays embrace the earth,
In every shadow, warmth and mirth,
Winds carry stories, old yet new,
Whispers dance in the vibrant hue.

Clouds drift lazily on high,
Painting dreams as we wander by,
Fields of gold spread far and wide,
In sunlit trails, our hearts confide.

Through open fields and meadows bright,
Nature's beauty sparks delight,
Chasing moments, fleeting and free,
Wandering souls, just you and me.

As the sun sets, colors collide,
In every heartbeat, joy resides,
Wandering through this perfect guise,
Together beneath the sunlit skies.

The Ebb and Flow of Bliss

In the dawn's soft glow, whispers weave,
Moments of joy, that we believe.
The tide retreats, yet leaves behind,
Embers of laughter that softly bind.

Seashells whisper secrets of old,
Stories of dreams and treasures bold.
With each new wave, hearts intertwine,
In the ebb and flow, our souls align.

Golden hues fade to a silver night,
Under the stars, our spirits take flight.
With every pulse, the ocean sings,
The rhythm of life, the happiness brings.

In twilight's embrace, we stand anew,
The journey unfolds, a vibrant hue.
As waves recede, they cradle our bliss,
In the dance of the tides, we find our kiss.

Enchanted Currents

Beneath the boughs where shadows play,
Enchanted currents sweep us away.
Each leaf a tale, each breeze a song,
In nature's arms, where we belong.

Water's glimmer, a silver lace,
Wraps us in a warm embrace.
With every ripple, secrets sigh,
In tranquil waters, worries die.

The sunlit path through golden glades,
Where whispers of magic softly invade.
An enchanted journey, hand in hand,
A world afresh, a promised land.

Wander we must, where dreams take flight,
Guided by stars in the velvet night.
Through the enchanted currents, we roam,
In nature's heart, we find our home.

Soaring on Silent Waves

In the hush of dawn, the silence blooms,
Soaring on waves, the heart consumes.
Up above clouds, where dreams reside,
In the stillness, our hopes collide.

Whispers of wind through the trees,
Carrying tales on fervent breeze.
Between the spaces where shadows lie,
We find the freedom, we learn to fly.

The azure skies stretch far and wide,
On silent waves, we take our ride.
With every heartbeat, we rise anew,
Soaring on paths where the wild things grew.

As starlight dances, the moon ignites,
Guiding our spirits through tranquil nights.
In the silent waves, we feel it all,
The beauty of life in a gentle call.

Floating on Mellow Rhapsodies

In twilight's hue, we drift and dream,
Floating on rhapsodies, it would seem.
Each note a whisper, soft and clear,
A melody lingers, inviting near.

Crimson skies fade to dusky gold,
Stories of love and hope unfold.
With every sigh, the world slows down,
In mellow tunes, we lose our frown.

Rippling waters, cradling peace,
A gentle embrace that will not cease.
Floating together where time unwinds,
In rhapsodic moments, connection binds.

As starlight twinkles on gentle waves,
We dance in whispers, the heart behaves.
Floating forever on music's flow,
In mellow rhapsodies, our spirits glow.

Borne of the Balmy Breeze

Soft whispers dance on the air,
Gentle sighs, a lover's care.
The sun dips low, its warm embrace,
Nature's kiss, a tranquil space.

Leaves sway lightly, shadows play,
In the dusk, dreams drift away.
Ebbing tides, the night unfurls,
Stars awaken, lighting worlds.

A fragrance sweet, of earth and sea,
Each moment wraps in harmony.
Borne aloft, in twilight's glow,
Heartbeats sync, as breezes flow.

In the calm, we find our peace,
Through the night, our worries cease.
Together here, we breathe, we please,
Borne of love, the balmy breeze.

Whimsy of the Wanderlust

Footprints scattered in the sand,
Stories lost, yet close at hand.
Fields of poppies, mountains high,
A distant land, beneath the sky.

Eager hearts, we chase the dawn,
In every path, a tale reborn.
Whimsy calls, we heed the song,
Adventure lures, we can't go wrong.

Cascading streams, and forest trails,
Following winds, where magic sails.
Maps unfurl, with dreams bestowed,
On wanderlust, our spirits flowed.

Moments stolen, laughter shared,
Through every journey, love declared.
With reckless joy, we roam the earth,
In every step, we find our worth.

Caressing the Gentle Undercurrents

Rippling waters, soft and shy,
Beneath the waves, life's lullaby.
Whispers drift on currents warm,
In the depths, we find the calm.

Silken tides, a smooth caress,
Nature's grace, in quietness.
Moonlit paths, where shadows glide,
In this world, our hearts confide.

Coral dreams and lantern light,
Guiding us through velvet night.
The ocean's breath, a tender sigh,
Caressing waves, as time slips by.

Here we linger, lost at sea,
In the rhythm, we long to be.
With every pulse, the world recedes,
Caressing all our silent needs.

The Calm Between the Storms

Dark clouds gather, whispers loom,
Yet in our hearts, a sense of bloom.
Before the thunder, stillness reigns,
A fleeting peace, where hope remains.

Winds may howl, and tempests roar,
Yet in stillness, we find the shore.
Gathering strength, we hold the line,
In the calm, our spirits shine.

Moments brief, yet deeply felt,
In muted breath, our fears do melt.
Upon the brink, we stand in awe,
The calm before, the world will draw.

Together here, we face the tides,
In every storm, our love abides.
For when the world is left to mourn,
We find our way, no heart forlorn.

Driftwood Stories on the Ocean's Edge

On the shore where tides collide,
Driftwood whispers secrets wide.
Each piece a tale of distant shores,
Carried by waves, it silently roars.

Beneath the skies, so vast and blue,
Stories lie in grains of dew.
The sun sets softly, painting the sand,
As life and wood find common land.

Footprints fade with the ebbing tide,
Memories linger, they cannot hide.
The ocean's breath, a timeless song,
Driftwood dreams where we belong.

In twilight's glow, the echoes play,
Carving paths in the twilight gray.
Through every splinter, life reclaims,
Driftwood stories whisper our names.

Sweet Escape of a Wandering Mind

In a field where daisies sway,
Clouds transform in a gentle play.
Thoughts drift softly like a breeze,
In the warmth, the heart finds ease.

Journeys taken on feathered wings,
In solace found, the spirit sings.
Amidst the chaos, a quiet space,
Where dreams dance with grace and pace.

Wandering paths of hidden dreams,
Flowing rivers, soft sunbeams.
Every glance, a tale untold,
In the heart, these moments hold.

As twilight falls, the stars align,
Within the silence, the soul can shine.
Escape, a gift from the mind's embrace,
Finding beauty in every place.

Harmonic Echoes Among the Vales

In valleys green where whispers soar,
Nature hums a lullaby's core.
Echoes dance through trees so tall,
Each note a memory, a call.

Rivers weave with a joyful glee,
Singing tales of harmony.
Mountains stand with ancient grace,
Guardians of this sacred place.

The breeze carries laughter from afar,
While fireflies twinkle, each a star.
In twilight's glow, the world is still,
Nature's song, a soothing thrill.

Amidst the silence, hearts unite,
In the magic of the night.
Harmonic echoes weave their spell,
A melody that weaves so well.

The Laughter of Leaves in the Afternoon

In golden light where shadows play,
Leaves giggle softly, swaying away.
Whispers rustle in the warm breeze,
Nature's joy, a song that frees.

Branches dance with a gentle cheer,
As sunlight filters, warm and clear.
Each flutter tells a story bright,
In the embrace of afternoon light.

The earth hums with life all around,
In laughter's echo, peace is found.
Barefoot steps upon the ground,
In leafy giggles, love is crowned.

As shadows stretch and daylight wanes,
The laughter lingers, joy remains.
In every leaf, a promise stays,
In the heart of nature's play.

Wandering Hearts in a Timeless Space

In the quiet dusk of fading light,
Two souls embark on dreams of flight.
Through whispers soft and glances shared,
They roam through realms no one has dared.

With every step in endless night,
They weave their hopes to heart's delight.
In laughter's echo, secrets grow,
A bond that only they can know.

The stars above, a watchful gaze,
Guiding their hearts through endless maze.
As time stands still, they dance in grace,
In wandering hearts, they find their place.

In timeless space their dreams align,
Forevers whispered, hearts entwined.
Together lost, together found,
In endless love, their souls resound.

Twilight's Embrace Beneath the Stars

As twilight falls, the world turns gold,
Embracing dreams and stories told.
The stars awaken, one by one,
In the blanket sky, the day is done.

With gentle breezes, night begins,
A serenade where silence spins.
In whispered wishes, hearts ignite,
Beneath the hush of falling night.

Luminous trails of twinkling light,
Guide wandering souls through endless night.
In this embrace, they find their voice,
In starlit realms, they freely rejoice.

Together lost 'neath cosmic glow,
In twilight's embrace, their spirits grow.
A dance of wonder, love's sweet art,
Forever held within the heart.

The Art of Serene Exploration

In tranquil paths, the journey flows,
With every step, the silence grows.
Through forests deep and mountains high,
The art of seeking dreams nearby.

Each leaf that rustles, every stream,
Invites the heart to softly dream.
With open eyes, the world unfolds,
In whispered tales, its beauty holds.

In quiet corners, wonders bloom,
The light of dawn dispels the gloom.
With every breath, a story's spun,
In serene exploration, they become one.

The path ahead, a canvas wide,
With every step, the soul's sweet guide.
In nature's arms, they'll find their way,
The art of life, in each new day.

Moments that Drift Like Autumn Leaves

In the golden glow of autumn skies,
Moments drift like whispered sighs.
A fleeting glance, a gentle breeze,
In these fragments, hearts find ease.

Leaves that twirl in vibrant dance,
Remind us all to take a chance.
With every rustle, time does weave,
The beauty found in what we leave.

Captured laughter, soft and sweet,
In cherished memories, lives complete.
Each thread of time, a story shared,
In autumn's embrace, we are bared.

Moments like leaves, they come and go,
A tapestry of warmth and glow.
As seasons turn, and time shall flow,
In hearts we hold them, ever so.

Ambrosial Escapes

In gardens where the wildflowers bloom,
Fragrant whispers dance on golden air,
A tapestry of colors in full plume,
Time bends softly, free from every care.

With every step, the earth sings sweet and low,
Cascading laughter from the brook nearby,
The sun paints shadows, basking in its glow,
As dreams of wanderlust take to the sky.

In twilight's glow, the starlight starts to wake,
Soft serenades weave through the night's embrace,
A fragrant chill as memories we make,
In ambrosial realms, we find our place.

With hearts unbound, we roam the endless trails,
Each moment lingers in the moonlit beams,
For in this haven, time forever pales,
Conceiving life anew through gentle dreams.

A Reverie on Liquid Dreams

Upon the lake, reflections shimmer bright,
A canvas drawn in ripples, soft and free,
The whispers of the wind paint tales of light,
    While echoes of the past drift quietly.

In silver waves, the moon begins to sway,
A siren's call in harmony so sweet,
Each drop a promise, beckoning to play,
In liquid dreams, where souls and echoes meet.

A symphony of stars in velvet skies,
As night unfurls its secrets, pure and clear,
With every twinkle, inspiration flies,
Each moment cherished, held forever near.

Awake in dreams, we soar through endless night,
Where all our visions merge in timeless streams,
As spirits dance on wings of sheer delight,
    In reveries, we sail on liquid dreams.

Lifting Spirits on Soft Winds

A breeze awakens whispers in the trees,
Carrying laughter, thoughts from far away,
With every gust, the heart feels light and free,
As spirits soar where earth and sky hold sway.

Through valleys deep, where wildflowers grow,
The wind caresses, gentle on our skin,
It sings of journeys, tales we long to know,
Inviting wanderers to breathe within.

As twilight deepens, colors start to blend,
A palette brushed by fleeting rays of sun,
Upon these waves, our sorrows start to mend,
Lifting spirits high, as day is done.

In twilight's grace, we turn to face the morn,
With hope renewed, each heart begins to sing,
For in these soft winds, we are reborn,
To touch the sky and feel the love they bring.

Harmony in the Hues of Dawn

As daybreak spills its colors through the trees,
A symphony awakens in soft light,
The horizon blushes, kissed by gentle breeze,
In harmony, the world prepares for flight.

Each note of nature sings a lullaby,
The rustling leaves join in with morning's glow,
Where shadows dance, and silences reply,
In hues of dawn, the magic starts to flow.

Golden rays embrace the dew-kissed ground,
As petals stretch and greet the waking day,
In each soft whisper, beauty can be found,
A canvas painted in the light of May.

So let us cherish every break of dawn,
For in its warmth, our hearts begin to bloom,
Embracing hope, as darkness slowly fades,
In harmony, we rise from shadows' gloom.

The Journey of a Feather on a Breeze

A feather drifts on gentle air,
Carried forth without a care.
It dances lightly, finds its way,
In whispers of the dawn of day.

Through sunlit fields and shadowed glades,
It glides where sunlight never fades.
In every swirl, a story spun,
Of journeys taken, dreams begun.

From tree to brook, from earth to sky,
It seeks the heights, it learns to fly.
Embracing grace, it floats and sways,
The world beneath in soft ballets.

At last it lands, a resting place,
A memory of its airy race.
In quiet stillness, it will stay,
A feather's journey fades away.

Embracing the Ease of a Soft Serenade

The night unfolds with gentle tunes,
As stars adorn the silver dunes.
A melody of whispered dreams,
In moonlit paths, the spirit gleams.

Each note flows soft like flowing streams,
Embracing all the heart's deep themes.
In every breath, a calm embrace,
The world retreats, a sacred space.

With every chord, the shadows pause,
Alive with nature's quiet cause.
The harmony of night unfurls,
Inviting peace in swaying curls.

As music fades, the dawn appears,
Yet still the serenade endears.
In echoes sweet, the night will stay,
A soft embrace that won't decay.

Reflections in a Pool of Calm

Beneath the trees, the water lies,
A mirror smooth, where silence sighs.
It captures all the sky's embrace,
Reflecting time in quiet space.

The leaves, they dance, in whispers near,
Rippling softly, crystal clear.
Each moment held in tranquil grace,
A fleeting world, a sacred place.

As clouds drift by, they cast their shade,
In stillness, life begins to wade.
A sacred pause, the heart may feel,
In this calm pool, the soul can heal.

And when the stars begin to glow,
The waters catch their softened show.
In every depth, a secret found,
Reflections timeless, thoughts unbound.

The Journey of Clouds in a Sky of Possibilities

The clouds embark on winds of chance,
In a sky where horizons dance.
They gather dreams, both big and small,
In wispy forms, they rise, they fall.

With every gust, they twist and turn,
A painter's touch, the heavens churn.
In light and shadow, tales unfold,
A canvas vast, in whispers told.

From white to gray, the colors blend,
They drift along, around the bend.
In storms they clash, in sunlight play,
A journey painted day by day.

And when the night begins to glow,
The stars emerge, their secrets show.
In endless skies, their dreams ignite,
The clouds, they wander through the night.

Milton Keynes UK
Ingram Content Group UK Ltd.
UKHW020044271124
451585UK00012B/1048

9 789916 906255